SOMETHING TO DISCUSS, REALLY IMPORTANT

SURAJ BOTHARA

THANK YOU

"FAMILY"

Contents

Preface

This book aims to discuss some topic which we generally passed or passing or will be passing in our life. It gives good insight about some feeling and emotion with whom we are connected and will be connected for life long. In short, rhymining sentence will make you connected throughout the poetic_story and you can have glimpse of, all your days once again which you ever experinced out ...

Acknowledgements

I thank, each and everyone who was/is a part of my life. Most importantly, i thank my FAMILY who is always there with me whenever i needed and gave freedom to me to do whatever i like to,so would like to ask to keep their hand on me forever. Meanwhile, would like to thank my MAAM and publication head for encouraging me to write more and publish my work. Moreover, my close friend were also part of my writing journey so would like to ask, do you mind being my friend for lifetime.

Prologue

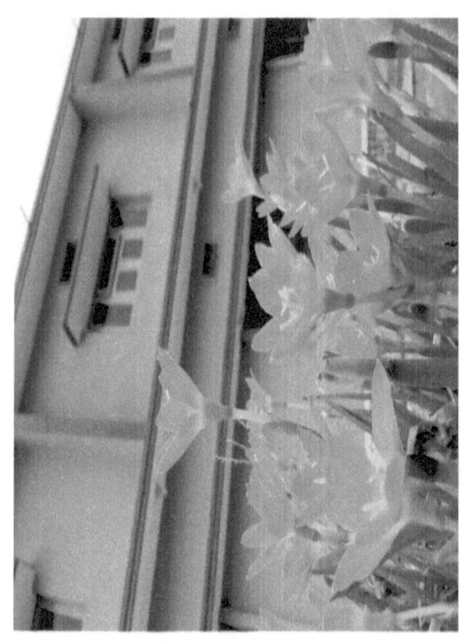

MOST BEAUTIFULL PLACE

1. Span Of "NINE AND HALF MONTH"

When I was residing inside your womb
*I had disturbed you multiple times, with **my kicks and boom***
Because I wanted another partner to talk and sing a rhyme
*And I found **you and your heaven** best place to spend time*
I was so excited that, I used to keep rolling up for comfort
*Perhaps my **unawareness** gave you multiple discomforts*

You always kept me as you first priority and hold me tight
*So that I could feel safe and say **everything is alright***
Whenever hurdle came, you shown your tolerance
*I wish I could perceive few **percent of it by inheritance***
In this situation, to do work and sustain was hard for sure
*But I was busy in growing mass as I was getting **everything***
pure
I assumed entire space is mine and wanted to walk mile
*But never bothered about your **pain behind your smile***

I lived like a king for several months in your province
*Where I was pampered and **you always try to convince***
I am very fortunate for finding your shelter to grow
*From where I could see **one more world** and say '**hello**'*
You always had believe on me and gave permission to flee
*Eventually, **your endurance** again helped me to come out and*

see

I know, no one in the world can justify your PENANCE
*So, better I love to **see your feet, and feel the essence.***
At last, you are adorable and will always be mine
*Since you gave me life, you are my **divine**…*

At present, I don't remember what all happened with me
But today's observation gave me some clue to agree
I cannot even predict, to what level of pain you might have

ramped
Because I had seen only 1-2 bones getting fractured and cramped
Thank you so much for bearing all those pains
I hope, my small cuddle will take off some strains …

"I believe, we can learn all lessons of life out of it
If we observe carefully this period with our grit. "

2. Few Words with "My MOTHER "

When I first opened my eyes on this earth
*I saw my mother face, she was **happy with my birth***
She took me in her hand, started staring at me
*Her **charming and loveable smile** pulled me to see*
I lied down on her hand for so many hours
*Perhaps, I was **deepening my bond** with her powers*
I slept ever night listening your melody sound
*Gave me sense of **calm and positive vibes** around*

She had different gestures to make me laugh
*Where I also enjoyed **every minute and half***
Yet, I wasn't able to walk and speak
*She could sense, which is **antique and unique***
Neither day nor night was easy for her
*Still she managed and **accepted my natural burr***
I made her irritated and disturbed, plenty of time
*She never left her hand rather **pushed me to climb***

One year of hard labour, promoted me to child
*My nature and characters both were **becoming wild***
I cried and hardly came in anyone's hand
*I loved you **lap**, didn't want to step in land*
When I started to walk on my knees
*Your joyful words attracted me to get **freeze***
I fell and shouted multiple times, during my peek
*You shown me path so that **I can streak***
*I made you to **run behind me**, carrying food*
This concludes how I passed my initial childhood.

Finally, day came when I was admission to school
*Early morning, she properly **dressed me with polished shoes***
She urged me to have breakfast slowly and completely
*Meanwhile, she packed my bag with water bottle **wholly***
With lots of smile in face, she dropped me in school van
*Occasionally, she came running with glass of **milk in hand***
***Mother**, your affection and love praised me to do works*
*Your angry nature also gave me, **multiple jerks**.*
You came earlier to me and don't want me to decline
*That is why you suggest me to **study well and shine**.*

I completed my 10th and brought smile in your face
*Your time was very crucial **to be in this place***
Everything I remember from breakfast to night drink
*Even observed during dark, waiting for my **last blink***
I went for my studies to nearby space
*It was hard for me to **stay away and brace***
Till today, you care about me and my life
*Although, completed my college life without any **strife***

Your prayers and believe were ultimate resource
*From where, I gained energy to **overcome every strokes***
Effective guidance and affectionate helped me to compile
*You believed on your upbringing and gave me **unique style***

*I am very happy and honored to get you as my **'MOTHER'***
*If miracle happens than I want to be in her, **to reborn***
further…

"THE MOST BEAUTIFUL AND DETERMINED
WOMEN IN THE WORLD"
"THANK YOU MUMMY"

3. Few Words With "My FATHER"

When I was born, I too shouted and cried
*I could sense, how happy you were **inside***
Father I am grown, looking at your face
*I never seen like you, **elegant and grace***
I am fortunate and glad, I am your part
*Share equal place with 'MOTHER', **in my heart***
When I succeed, I will remain down-to-earth like others
*I need your **hand on my head** along with mother*

You fulfilled our entire wish
*Brought everything in **single dish***
You gave us everything before we ask
*You never shown, kept it **behind mask***
I had guilt; I didn't spend more time before
*Now I realized, your were ascertaining our **needs of store***
I was child and you wanted me to shine like a star
*Accordingly, your every step were **optimistic and far***

You didn't get time to realize, when day passed and night went
*Entire life, you dedicated in building our **future and present***
I remember those frozen hands and running sweat
*Which you faced during struggle days, to clear **debt***
Many a days, you had your food unplanned
***Rigorous work** didn't gave you time to understand*
*I had seen your **dedication to work** and **selfless nature** with*
us
*Your journey is sufficient for **upcoming generation** to discuss*

I hardly remember when I told you about me
*Rather than **casual talks**, I hope you agree*
You gave all freedoms which was necessary for my age
*Never had any issue, with whomever I **engaged***
I took it in grant, sometimes disobeyed
*I know your image, with whom I was **afraid***
*Till today I **feel fear**, will be continued ahead*
*As long as, I leave the air and take **rest on bed***

Fortunately, I am blessed to have you as my **'FATHER'**
I am sure your **sacraments**; *help me stand out from others*
I know, no one in the world can justify your PENANCE
So better, I love to **see your feet and feel the essence.**
Lastly, I don't know what will happen in time ahead
You will see my head, always **bowing you down** *as I said...*

"THE MOST CHALLENGING AND HONEST MAN IN
THE WORLD"
"THANK YOU PAPPA"

4. Few Words To "INSPIRE"

Somebody's life is messed and cornered
*Don't you think, need some more **time to think off***
How about you make your next attempt
*Which you left behind for **some reason***
Conquer it, with some more spirit and labour
***Embarrass your participation,** on bringing it towards your*
favor

Always keep personifying your dream
*Don't hesitate for your **next scream***
Insanity takes you towards you lane
*When more your **struggle** and suffer the **pain***
Wisely choose your path and get into it to play
*Don't stop yourself until you **find it on your way***

When you come across many choices in your life
*Stick to one and start piercing it **with your multiple strives***
Faith and believe are two major thing to understand
*Individual patience and tolerance, will land you to **success's***
hand
Salute to those who are loyal and optimism
*Because happy ending happens only **in the hand of deserving***
one's

Few get's inspiration early in life and others in later stage
*Problems is, difficult **to perceive in daily's life** hence, remains*
in cage
Don't lose hope until you receive your answer
*This might be the question of your life, giving you a **pressure***
Passing life will be easy once you identify yourself in light
*Or else you might be one, who will be **roaming in dark night***

In life, failure and success comes one after another
So better wait for your time and keep trying further....

5. Few Words On "BROTHER AND SISTER BOND"

I don't know how to start
*There are **plenty of things in my cart***
Every single time that I passed with her
*It was **full of joy and with some harsh***
It may sound as if, it is common to all
*Perhaps, everyone admires the **strength in this bond.***

Every relation has unique way to express
*This is the one which remains **every time clean and fresh***
I don't need to convince you all about this relation
*Still, I will add up few with **some prescription***
Emphasis on this pristine and instinct connection
***Start mesmerizing** with me, on my down collection.*

Whether she is born before or after our birth
*She inherits and possesses **rights on us***
We quarreled and fought for every single thing
*We even had jealousy for **not getting any thing***
Those days were belonged to her
*But we were **happy for being the part of all***
May, we opted for getting something in return
*Perhaps, she was the reason **behind that curtain.***

Sad and dull came between us at every instant
*But we didn't **make it to last long and maintain distant***
Basically, we opt to fight with her rather than securing
*Because these were the memories which **started building***
Crying, shouting, and enacting are the rhymes of our day to day
life
*May be because, her sound fulfills our **blank and side.***

Honestly, we felt alone when she didn't talk
*Such a **bold attachment** we possess with her*
We can neglect and forgive thousands of mistakes
*But it' our duty to **show path and make her awake***
May I won't be the good advisor or guider
*But to my extent, I will always be with her as a **well wisher.***

Finally, these doesn't end with these short note
*There is much more to come in the **next stroke***
I am making an appeal with all brothers and sisters
*Sorrows and happy do comes **with some purpose***
Stay calm and believe in your relation
*No need to receive **other's suggestion.***

Till now life is being too long and memories aside
Keep playing your inning and enjoy your ride.

6. Few Words On "Farmers life"

This is the story about, distinct man
*Who lives in a small house, with **limited plan***
They don't have other reasons to survive except for us
*Hence we should understand, they have only one option in **each***
toss
I don't need to explain about their roles and responsibility
*Data explains, they account **one-third of world's GDP**,*
exclusively
*I feel **honor and happy** to write on it and present*
May be these would be my small tribute with genuine intent

Here we go---à
Let's start from beginning of the season
*Where he carries instruments and wear **white turban***
Along with few animals, he walks towards his farm
Meanwhile he makes a glance on his field and expresses his
charm
He starts plouging and irrigating as per his need

*So it took him time to attain, good atmosphere and **spread
seed***
Even though his legs in mud, he starts sowing sapling one by one
*Astonishing is that, he loves to talk although it's **scorching
sun**...*

Every day and night he works to safeguard his farm
*Never made a compromise although it was **cool, rainy or
warm***
At one period of time, he harvest crops and brings down to sell
*Where his punctuality and work ethics has to **pay him well***
*After a long journey of, **hard work** and **determination***
*He experiences the feeling of **relaxation** and **satisfaction***

For a while, stress and burden comes down to rest
*That's how they run their family and enjoy like a **fest***
*On other side, there are many farmers, who **disperse and suffer***
Tens to hundred reasons behind that to occur
Many lost their life and becomes homeless
*Because they could not able to pay their loans and **express
restless***
They stay away from joy and happiness for sometime
*If nobody works on it, then it's going to **harm others** for
lifetime.*

Whenever I hear the news of damage crops
*I pray for their family, to give them strength and **show them***
props
*I know, I cannot bring them out from their **pain and sorrow***
I believe, my pray will work for them tomorrow
*They are the reason behind **our survival***
*So we should be proud and show **respect for their arrival**…*

Lastly, I just wanted to appeal, if you would like
*Before you eat, just **recall them and pray** for a while*
Individual pray can form a big chain
*If you really think we need to **share their pain.***

*SALUTE TO ALL THOSE REAL HEROES -à **"FARMERS"***

7. Few Words On "Student life"

When I step into the student life for the first time
*I found many pillars and some **people around***
I had believe that, this institution will bless my fate
*So I received admission **without any hate***
Keeping in mind that I am going to be part of it
*Accordingly I started planning, arranging all my **essential kit***
To some extent I was frighten, how college and friends be like
*After a while, I **stop anticipating** and kept it aside*

Day came when I actually started my journey
*I had doubt, why everybody's face is **full of queries***
It took me time to understand why it is so
Perhaps, I was also suffering from the same and wanted to
approach
Honestly, it wasn't difficult to interact and mingle
*Because they just **need, 'Hello'** and **cool behavior***

By then I had plenty of friends to talk
*Among them **few are soft and some are rock***
Once you started spending time with them
*You will feel strange to work on yourself and your **strength***
Slowly I understood, importance of their presence
*Because many believe it's just few years, **to sustain***
I would suggest, never take study and friends for grant
*Meanwhile, you work on both and find your **confidant***

❧❧❧

In college life, you will be passing more time with your classmates
***Sharing** your lunch box and **laughing** at some non-sense*
You may even fight for small-small things,
*It won't matter because these are going to be **daily scenes***
There will be few who want to show off and grab attention
*Few wishes to show their strength and give other's **tension***
Meanwhile, some of will come with explicit mind set
*Similarly, few come to **flourish and increase** their strength*

❧❧❧

During this period, you will go through from different scene
*Where teachers will be **scolding** and you will be listening*
There will be some friends, disturbing and murmuring from
behind When teacher asks, they start pointing but never reveals
mastermind
Few friends will eagerly waiting for such shoot

*So that they can hide themselves and **engulf little bit food***

There will be plenty of days where you will enjoy
*Because, student life will be full of fest and **envoy***
I would suggest, participate in few or more events
*Where you think, you can **boost and sharp** your sense*
Never think about, how other will react
*Believe me, there will be few who will **appreciate your track***
You will feel kind of satisfaction after your enrollment
*Moreover, you won't **regret in future**, will do less accidents*

I won't suggest you to stay with rankers or poor scorers
*Because everyone has **unique way** to hustle and find their*
careers
These many years you will be working on yourself
*Try to come out with distinct nature, **without proving others***
You should feel, you have earn something during these tenure
*It won't matter if you don't, because there is lot to **come in***
future..

After a long journey, teacher announces for a farewell date
*Where you start missing friends, teachers, and **college gate***
Everyone will be busying in sharing the means of connection
*But very few realize and feel the **pain of separation***
Nevertheless, I just want college life to be memorable for you
*So do whatever you like which **favors for you.***

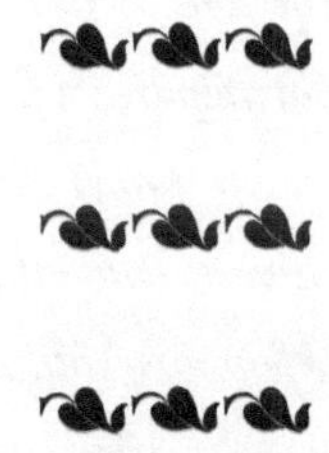

"Till now life is being too long and memories aside
Keep playing your inning and enjoy your ride….."

8. A THANKFUL NOTE TO ALL MY 'FRIENDS'

I want all of you to applaud and cheers for this relation
*It has deep and intense feeling with **lots of admiration!***
When I pen down, I was laughing and even being emotional
*Because all memories were so **graceful and additional***
I start mesmerizing, all my day before memories
*Where I was **moving fearlessly** and eating near bakeries*
These would be a small thankful note to my entire peers
*Who are far, but still **feel they are near***

I had spent best of my time along with creating content
*Where I **explored** myself, from minute to possible extent*
I mean, I started enjoying and learning side by side
*It was also there hand, who gave **direction to my tide***
I am still amaze, how I grew up my friendship
*But, I express my gratitude for being there during my **hardship***
I am very thankful and pleased for this opportunity
*Because this relation has **strengthen my immunity***

*Real friends are literally **blessings** for few*
*Who admires **it's sublime** and keeps faith in them as true*
Friendship means, you don't expect anything in return
*Instead, it teaches us the meaning of **"concern"***
Sharing my food and sorrows with them today
*Has helped me to collect memories **for my midway***
Till today I don't feel low and deficient
*Because I believe my **one gesture** is sufficient…*

True friendship never ends, unless you wish or revert
But you can refrain for sometime if you get hurt.

F- Fearless

R-Relation

I-Immortalizes

E-Emotionally,

N-Never

D-Dying

S-Soul

9. Few Words On "Solitude"

Why you should admire:
This is the beautiful feeling to admire and realize
*But very few **perceive and relax** their mind pipes*
Happy and sad are quiet stop for a while
*Sounding peace will make you to **believe from inside***
It will give you a break to refresh
*You are supposed to find yourself and **your self respect.***

Causes:
Plenty of reason to fall under this issue
*One may be your **ignorance** and other may be your **attitude***
Honestly, you may have lost the connection
*Which you were supposed to handle and **gain it with your affection***
You may get hurt by someone's action and incident
*By then you may find easy way **to stay far from them.***

Impact:
You may feel low and armless
Stage of oblivious and senseless
Regretting inside and shouting with a deep cry
*No need of extra emotion, it's just a waste of **precious time***
Coherently, everyone's life is concerned and connected with
loneliness
*Or else how will you mean the **importance of togetherness.***

Suggestion:
Make yourself busy with different stuff
*Mingle with someone and become **hard and tough***
Don't make it to last, for long run
*Because, it's harmful for **every single one***
It may be part of your life
*Welcome it, with our **decent smile.***

Opinion:

*We should **respect and honor** for its existence*
For being so mean throughout its presence
It possess both pros and cons
Matter of the fact is essential to come
It doesn't matter whether you find yourself or not
But you will experience this strange one.

10. Summarizing Entire "Life journey"

*This is a **rhyme,** that attempt and convey you all*
It talk about the stage that you might, experienced out
*Every **struggle and phase,** we may feel out*
Finally took out time and made a note to revel it out
This would be the toughest one, which you ever dealt with
But I assure you, I will make you feel connected through out of
it.

When you grew from infant to child
You had someone to hold and make you walk alongside
*This was a period when you **never shattered***
Did you ever amaze how easily it occurred?
Licking finger and struggling to walk
*There was someone fluttering around and **showing you path.***

When you travel the age from child to boy
*You start feeling the **workload** side by side*
Study is the main part at this point
*Where you may suffer and **touch the peak height***
When everybody race for the position
*Very few, **urges to flourish** and nurture the situation*
Physical and mental growth happens at this stage
***Gaming and building relations** is the only reason behind this*
age.

❧❧❧

When someone feel the age of maturity
*There is lot more **to learn and emphasize**, without any*
insecurity
You will face happy, sad and loneliness
*But you should try **not to land in emptiness***
There are feeling and emotions that you need to respect for
*Meanwhile **try to inherit** and be the perfect one.*

❧❧❧

When anyone falls in age of responsibility
*It teaches you to **tackle condition and possibility***
*Life will take different turns, where **ups and down** will be*
common
***Affectionate, caring, patience and love** are the one to*
summon

Avoid distraction which utters your path and foot
*Be very focus and concentrate on your **next shoot***
Fill up your all space, keeping next step in your mind
*Never listen to other who **harms you mankind***
Your strength could be family and relation
*Always adhere to it and **bring it to profession.***

Last but not the least stage, closer to bed
*Where you have only **mental strength** to use ahead*
Here, you experience talks a bit louder
*Thereafter **plenty of things** to speak out with others*
Mesmerizing the every stage of life's quagmire
*Inheriting and dealing with the next **holder of 'EMPIRE'***

*Remembering the names of god and **embracing the heaven***
*He/she starts to compile it in a book, with **title life lesson.***
***RIP** would be the very small word to respect, one's life*
*Who one or the other day **entertained** someone's side*
*Make sure you walk on **righteous path** shown by them*
*Never betray yourself or else you will **feel shame***
Do the things, where someone remember you for the good one
*Bring the **smile in one's face** which sticks to it and so on.*

Short Description

My name is SuRaj Bothara. I completed my primary education from NEPAL and doing my further studies from INDIA. I developed interest for writing rhyming sentences meanwhile i realised, i can write the stories from rhyming sentences as well so, with due determination and time i was able to discuss 10 topics as you read from starting. I believe you liked it and wish to get showered with love further in future .

I wish good health and happy ending for all.

THANK YOU